QUICK JOB SUCCESS GUIDE

Seven Steps to Getting Ahead on the Job

**The Editors at JIST
with Contributions by Michael Farr**

Contents

Step 1: Put Your Best Foot Forward from the Start 1
Step 2: Learn All You Can About Your Job 10
Step 3: Develop Your People Skills 16
Step 4: Make the Right Choices 26
Step 5: Build on Your Reputation 32
Step 6: Create a Career Plan 35
Step 7: Position Yourself to Get Ahead 44

Quick Job Success Guide Is Short, But It May Be All You Need

This quick, activity-filled workbook gives you tools and ideas to help you keep your new job and even prepares you for better jobs beyond this one. Why is that important?

An online poll of more than 20,000 people reported that 86 percent were not satisfied with their jobs. Work rates as a priority in our lives because it's how we support ourselves. We earn money to pay for a place to live, a car to drive, the food we eat, the clothes we wear, and the education we provide to our children.

But work is more than that. It's also how we build our self-esteem and feel good about ourselves. It's how we learn to build relationships with people who have different backgrounds or points of view. Work teaches us, motivates us, and gives us a chance to learn and grow. Furthermore, we spend more time at work than any other single activity in our busy lives.

There's no doubt that work is important to us. That's why finding and keeping a good job matters. You want to be the kind of employee who

- Gets along with others on the job
- Earns the best pay you can for your position
- Is chosen for training
- Receives recognition and promotions
- Feels proud of your performance

That's what we emphasize in *Quick Job Success Guide*.

Trust Us—Do the Worksheets. We know you will resist completing the worksheets. But trust us. They are worth your time. Doing them will give you a better sense of what you are doing well, what you need to improve, and how to go about making those improvements. You will also most likely get more responsibilities and present yourself better. Is this worth giving up a night of TV? Yes, we think so.

Once you finish this booklet and its activities, you will have spent more time planning your career than most people do. And you will know more than the average employee about succeeding on the job.

Why Such a Short Book? We are often been asked to tell someone, in a few minutes or hours, the most important things they should do to be successful on the job. Instructors and counselors also ask the same question because they have only a short time to spend with folks they're trying to help. We've given this a lot of thought, and the seven topics in this booklet are the ones we think are most important to know.

This booklet is short enough to scan in an evening and start a new job the next day. Granted, doing all the activities would take more time, but they will prepare you far better than scanning the book. Of course, you can learn more about all the topics it covers, but this booklet, *Quick Job Success Guide*, may be all you need.

We wish you well.

The Editors at JIST

Michael Farr

The Seven Steps for Quick Job Success

Good job! You survived the interview process, impressed all the right people, and got the job. You might think the hard part is over and you can relax. That couldn't be more wrong. Finding the right job is hard work. Keeping it can be even harder—but only when you're not prepared.

This book is organized around seven steps that are most important for job success:

1. Put your best foot forward from the start.
2. Learn all you can about your job.
3. Develop your people skills.
4. Make the right choices.
5. Build on your reputation.
6. Create a career plan.
7. Position yourself to get ahead.

Take the time to read the information and complete the worksheets for each of the seven steps in this booklet. Think about the examples and learn as much as you can as you go through the book. Step-by-step, you'll find simple, commonsense ways to keep your job and even get ahead.

STEP 1: Put Your Best Foot Forward from the Start

The good news is that you have the ability to avoid many problems by how you prepare yourself and what you do in your daily job performance. This is especially true when you are just beginning a new job. You're starting fresh. You're excited and full of hope. The person who hired you feels the same way. You both want to prove that the decision to hire you was wise. So let's review how you can put yourself in the best position to be happy and successful in your job.

The Three Major Employer Expectations

First, you must understand what your boss wants from you. In general, most managers have three major expectations of employees:

- **Dependability.** Can you be depended on to be reliable and to do a good job for a reasonable length of time?
- **Appearance.** Do you look like the type of person who will succeed on the job and readily fit in with the other people in the organization?
- **Skills.** Do you have the necessary training, experience, skills, and credentials to do the job?

You must be honest with yourself. Do you meet your employer's expectations? If not, what can you do to become the type of employee your supervisor wants?

Why People Get Fired

Another way to think about how to succeed comes from thinking about why people *don't* succeed. For example, take a look at this list of reasons people lose their jobs:

1. Could not get along with other workers
2. Proved to be dishonest (lied or stole things)
3. Did not have acceptable appearance or grooming
4. Was unreliable, too many days absent or late
5. Used work time for personal business
6. Could not do the work
7. Worked too slowly, made too many mistakes
8. Refused to follow orders
9. Misrepresented skills or experience
10. Did not follow safety rules

Do you have trouble with any of the preceding issues? Would your former supervisors use any of those reasons to describe your employment history? Many worksheets and examples in this booklet can help you avoid these problems.

Watch Your Attitude

You may just be starting out at a new job or wanting to improve your performance on your current job. Like it or not, other people—your boss, your co-workers, and your customers—will definitely be looking at you, judging you. They're trying to make up their minds whether you fit into their workplace. Your words, your gestures, and your actions will tell them everything they need to know.

To succeed, you have to work smart. And the first thing that needs your attention is your attitude. Look again at the list of reasons employees get fired. Did you notice that attitude is a major part of so many items on the list?

Think about it. Working with others is a lot like trying to make friends with someone you really like. You want to make a good impression, and you want the other person to like you. So you take extra care in getting dressed. You smile. You are polite. You do everything you can to let the other person know you want to get along.

Your job is just like that. Every day you go to work, you are expected to have an acceptable attitude and get along with the people who cross your path. Checking your attitude every so often can help you stay on the track to success. Are you ready to make a good impression, or does your attitude need a tune-up?

CHECK YOUR ATTITUDE	
Place a checkmark in front of the following attitudes you know you have.	
❏ Arrive early and stay late	❏ Be defensive
❏ Smile and be friendly	❏ Complain
❏ Ask for more responsibility	❏ Interrupt others
❏ Volunteer to help others	❏ Make promises that cannot be kept
❏ Learn on your own time	❏ Gossip
❏ Ask for more training	❏ Blame others
❏ Accept new assignments willingly	❏ Ignore others
❏ Encourage others' ideas	❏ Act like a know-it-all
❏ Accept help from others	❏ Put tasks off to the last minute

You may have noticed that the first column has positive attitudes and the second, negative ones. Which column did you check most often? Read on for tips on overcoming negative attitudes.

Work Toward Having a Good Attitude

If you need immediate help with a negative attitude, try following these tips:

- **Use breathing to calm you down.** Pulling your stomach muscles in and out five to ten times usually brings oxygen into your body and gives you a chance to calm down.

- If your work environment allows it, you may want to take a quick walk outside, look out a window, or take a moment to write your feelings and thoughts in a journal.

- Make sure that you take good care of your body and relationships. Getting plenty of sleep, eating good foods, exercising, and spending time with people who care about you can change your attitude over time.

Everyone Needs a Little Help Sometimes

If those healthy lifestyle behaviors don't improve your attitude, you may want to see a counselor. Many employers offer counseling services to their employees—even those who are just joining the organization.

If you know before you even begin a job that you have a negative attitude, take action on your own. You can explore the following sources for help:

- Check with agencies in your local community or your telephone book for counselors who offer mental health services. Some are free.

- Search the Internet for articles on maintaining a positive attitude.

- Look through the books and recordings in your local library or bookstore for self-help materials.

- Talk with a trusted friend, family member, or someone from your church about overcoming a negative attitude.

- Keep a private journal in which you can write freely about your feelings.

Ultimately, your attitude is your responsibility, and you can control it. Ignore your negative attitude, and you may find yourself looking for another job sooner than you might want.

> **Quip**
>
> A positive attitude is good for your health. Not only is a good attitude important in keeping a job, it's also important to your health. According to a study reported in *The Journal of the American Medical Association,* the higher people score on tests of impatience and hostility during young adulthood, the more likely they are to develop high blood pressure later in life.

Pay Attention to How You Look

Whether you agree or not, your dress and grooming communicate a message to others. For example, your appearance tells everyone around you whether you want to fit in or stand out.

Think About What You Wear on the Job

Some workplaces have written dress codes, but many do not. When you have questions about what is okay and what isn't, look around. To make a good impression, look for people who are doing well at your workplace and try to dress and groom in a similar way. If you are not sure, dress a little better than your co-workers, particularly in a new job. Wear clean and well-pressed clothing and pay particular attention to your grooming and other details, like your shoes.

THE DRESS CODE IN YOUR WORKPLACE

To help you figure out what is acceptable, place a checkmark beside the type of clothing that is allowed at your workplace.

- ❑ Blue jeans
- ❑ Dress pants or slacks
- ❑ Khaki or casual pants
- ❑ Button-down shirts or blouses
- ❑ Pullover shirts
- ❑ Dresses or skirts
- ❑ Tennis shoes or sneakers
- ❑ Business suits with ties
- ❑ Casual or soft-soled shoes
- ❑ Dress shoes or high heels
- ❑ Jewelry

If employees at your workplace are required to wear safety or protective wear, place a checkmark beside the article(s) required.

- ❑ Apron
- ❑ Gloves
- ❑ Goggles or protective eyewear
- ❑ Hair covering
- ❑ Hard hat
- ❑ Hearing protection
- ❑ Lab coat
- ❑ Steel-toed footwear

If employees at your workplace wear uniforms, place a checkmark under the correct answer for the following questions.

Yes No

- ❑ ❑ Is the uniform provided by the employer?
- ❑ ❑ Is there a uniform cost you must pay?

(continued)

(continued)

> ❑ ❑ Is the uniform available at the workplace?
>
> ❑ ❑ Do you need the uniform before your first day?
>
> ❑ ❑ Are you responsible for the cleaning and care of your uniform?
>
> List the specific items that are part of the uniform. _____
>
> _____
>
> _____

Personal Grooming Is Important

Little things really matter when it comes to fitting in with a work group. Your personal grooming affects your attitude and the way others act toward you. When you look the best you can, you feel better about yourself. When you feel better about yourself, your attitude and relationships with others improve.

Make sure that you take a daily shower or bath, groom your hair, wear clean clothes and shoes, wear little or no cologne, use deodorant, and limit your jewelry.

Work to Get Rid of Negative Habits

Most of us have one or more habits that bother others but that we may not even be aware of. For example, some people say "Know what I mean" or "Uh" as they speak. Others may play with their hair, shake a foot, avoid looking up when they speak, or have other annoying habits.

Think about your negative habits. Be brave enough to ask your family, friends, and former co-workers for their opinions. The following worksheet can help you figure out whether you have any habits that could prevent you from fitting in at your job.

> ### CHECK YOUR HABITS
>
> Following is a list of common bad habits. Can you name others? Place a checkmark beside any behaviors that you have, and then do your best to change your bad habits into good ones.
>
> ❑ Bragging   ❑ Burping
>
> ❑ Asking co-workers for money   ❑ Borrowing without asking

- ❏ Chewing or popping gum
- ❏ Chewing with an open mouth
- ❏ Fidgeting
- ❏ Checking personal e-mail or surfing on the Web
- ❏ Drumming fingers or tapping foot
- ❏ Interrupting others
- ❏ Grunting or mumbling answers
- ❏ Taking personal phone calls
- ❏ Nagging
- ❏ Playing music too loud
- ❏ Name-dropping
- ❏ Treating others rudely
- ❏ Selling products at work
- ❏ Stealing
- ❏ Sharing intimate personal details
- ❏ Swearing
- ❏ Singing in an open work area
- ❏ Talking too loud
- ❏ Spitting
- ❏ Telling lies
- ❏ Frequently having bad breath
- ❏ Frequently arriving late
- ❏ Grooming in the work area
- ❏ Frequently being absent
- ❏ Biting fingernails
- ❏ Gambling
- ❏ Not bathing
- ❏ Making personal phone calls
- ❏ Procrastinating
- ❏ Wearing too much perfume or cologne
- ❏ Complaining
- ❏ Taking too many or long breaks
- ❏ Ridiculing or ignoring others' ideas
- ❏ Not accepting responsibility for mistakes
- ❏ Always claiming to be right
- ❏ Threatening others
- ❏ Criticizing others
- ❏ Whining

Others: _____

_____

_____

You can change any negative behaviors or attitudes if you first admit that you have the habit and then spend some time thinking about these two questions:

- What are you getting by having the habit?
- What are you losing by having the habit?

For every habit, there is a payoff and a tradeoff—the good and bad that happen when you repeat a habit. Saying "Know what I mean" or "Uh" may give you time to think about what you will say next, but what is the tradeoff? What kind of impression do those words create?

After you have recognized that you have a negative habit and its positive and negative results, you are more likely to replace the negative habit with a good one. If you realize that you are always critical, the way to stop is to consciously look for the good in others. Making the change may seem uncomfortable at first, but experts say that if you continue to practice the positive behavior for 30 days, you can create a new habit and leave the negative one behind.

PLAN TO OVERCOME NEGATIVE HABITS

Use the following worksheet to create a plan to overcome one negative habit. If you want to correct other negative habits and find this process helpful, get some paper and repeat the process for each habit.

1. The negative habit you want to overcome is _____

2. Your payoff for continuing the negative habit is _____

3. The tradeoff for continuing the negative habit is _____

4. The new behavior you want to use to overcome the negative one is _____

5. The date by which you will work toward overcoming this habit is _____

If you were able to overcome your habit by the date you set, congratulations! If not, don't give up. Changing a habit takes patience. Be patient with yourself and try again.

Know Your Work Schedule

When you have a job, you need to plan ahead so that you can be at work when you are scheduled. The worksheet that follows can help you plan ahead to avoid being late or other problems that can get in the way of working.

PLAN YOUR DAILY SCHEDULE

In the lines provided, write the hour that you need to complete each of the following tasks. Then look for problems that may occur in your daily schedule.

What Time Do You Need To	Time
Be at work?	_____
Take or send the children in your care (if any) to daycare or school?	_____
Catch the bus, train, or carpool?	_____
Leave home?	_____
Prepare meals before work?	_____
Wake other family members?	_____
Be in the shower or bath?	_____
Wake up?	_____

In the following lines, list the potential problems in your daily routine that could make you late to work. Then write what you need to do to overcome each problem.

Potential Problem	Plan to Overcome It
_____	_____
_____	_____
_____	_____
_____	_____
_____	_____
_____	_____
_____	_____

Seven Quick Steps to Solving Problems

Do you have trouble solving problems? Use the following seven steps to find the best solution to those problems that you face.

1. **Define the problem.**

   For example, you have trouble getting to work on time.

2. **List the causes of the problem.**

   To continue the example, the reason you're late is that you never hear the alarm. The reason that you don't hear the alarm, however, is because you stay up until 1 or 2 a.m. working a second job.

3. **List possible solutions.**

   In the example, one solution is to get a louder alarm. Another is to ask a friend or relative to call you every morning. A third solution is to quit your second job.

4. **Analyze each of the solutions.**

   In analyzing the possible solutions, you realize that a louder alarm may not make a difference. Asking a friend or relative to call you puts the burden on the other person—and you still might not wake up. Quitting the second job is impossible; you need the money to pay the bills.

5. **Choose the best solution.**

   Probably the best solution is to get a louder alarm.

6. **Take action.**

7. **Evaluate whether you solved the problem.**

   You'll know in just a few days whether the solution to get a louder alarm worked.

STEP 2: Learn All You Can About Your Job

Sometimes we are tempted to think that graduating from a program or getting a job means that we are finished, that the learning is over. For the person who wants to succeed, learning must never end. The successful person thinks about and chooses ways to continue learning throughout life.

Identify Skills You Need to Improve

Every job requires a variety of skills an employee must have to do it well. Some of these are job-specific, such as the software knowledge and skills an accountant must have or the training a fire fighter must have. But there are a variety of other skills employees need to succeed. Use the worksheet on the next page to identify areas where you need to improve your skills.

SKILLS YOU NEED TO IMPROVE

List the skills that you need for your job. For each skill, place a checkmark in the column that most clearly defines your need for additional skill development. Place a checkmark under "Adequate" if your skill in this area is good enough to allow you to function well on this job. Place a checkmark under "Need to Improve" if you need to improve this skill to keep or move ahead on this job.

Your Job Title or Type of Job: _____

Job-Specific Skills	Adequate	Need to Improve
_____	☐	☐
_____	☐	☐
_____	☐	☐
_____	☐	☐
_____	☐	☐

Specific Equipment to Operate	Adequate	Need to Improve
_____	☐	☐
_____	☐	☐
_____	☐	☐
_____	☐	☐
_____	☐	☐

Math, Science, Technology Skills	Adequate	Need to Improve
_____	☐	☐
_____	☐	☐
_____	☐	☐
_____	☐	☐
_____	☐	☐

(continued)

(continued)

People Skills	Adequate	Need to Improve
_____	☐	☐
_____	☐	☐
_____	☐	☐
_____	☐	☐
_____	☐	☐

Any Other Skills or Personality Traits Important in This Job	Adequate	Need to Improve
_____	☐	☐
_____	☐	☐
_____	☐	☐
_____	☐	☐
_____	☐	☐

When you finish this list, go back and circle the five skills you think are most important for you to improve on in order to succeed in this job. Then decide on a date by which would you like to acquire each of those skills.

Take Advantage of On-the-Job Training

Your job may be familiar because of your past work experience, or it may be entirely new to you. Either way, you need to learn specific things to do *this* job well. Some employers have formal training programs to get new employees started. Others expect you to learn on your own.

Look for the learning opportunities your organization offers and take advantage of them. Often, you will be able to learn new skills at little or no cost. And everything you learn for this job prepares you for your next one and for your career.

A transferable skill is a skill that is not job-specific. Transferable skills are ones you can apply to many different jobs, even in other industries. For example, you must use a computer keyboard in an office, but you also use it for operating store cash registers, running a warehouse inventory system, making police reports, or even checking cars into a quick oil lube garage. Look for the transferable skills you can learn in your workplace and take with you wherever you go.

Talk with your manager about the training options your employer offers. Use the following worksheet to identify the training resources available for your job.

THE RESOURCES THAT ARE AVAILABLE TO YOU

Place a checkmark beside the resources your employer offers new employees.

- ❏ Job description
- ❏ Working with assigned co-worker
- ❏ Computer classes
- ❏ New employee orientation program
- ❏ Policy and procedures manual
- ❏ Watching other employees or work groups
- ❏ In-service training classes
- ❏ Formal training with a manager or supervisor
- ❏ Outside training or education

You can learn a great deal and avoid many mistakes by paying attention to the information your employer makes available. If you can benefit from specific outside training, tell your supervisor how the training will help your work, volunteer to teach what you learn to other workers, and ask if the organization will pay you for the training.

Connect with Others

When you're new on a job or shy, you will probably feel a little out of place. You don't know the people there or the way to get things done. What can you do to begin to feel at home in your surroundings? Here are some tips to help you connect with your coworkers and figure out what to do:

- Don't be afraid to introduce yourself to people you don't know.
- Tell others that you are new on the job or a little shy.
- Ask other people about what they do and how your job relates to theirs.
- Observe others carefully. Pay attention to how they do their work; how they relate to their supervisors, co-workers, and other people they come in contact with on the job; and their attitudes.

Most people want to help, so don't hesitate to ask for help or information when you need to understand how a piece of equipment operates, what to do with certain paperwork when it's finished, and so on.

Where can you go to learn the skills you don't have right now if others cannot or will not help you? In an ideal world, your supervisor and every co-worker would try to help those who need to learn new skills. Unfortunately, that is not always the case.

If you have little or no help in learning the basics at your job, you may want to take the following actions to learn the needed skills on your own:

- Use career references or search the Internet for information on the skills you need for your job.
- Check with schools in your community for courses on topics you can use on the job, such as computers or languages.
- Look for community groups that meet to support and educate their members.

Pay Attention to the Money

Most of us expect to be paid for the work we do, and chances are great that you do, too. You will want to be aware of these points, particularly as you begin a new job:

- The amount of pay you are to receive
- The amount of money the employer will deduct from your pay
- The additional benefits the employer may give

Be Aware of Taxes and Benefits

The employer probably will be required to deduct these taxes from your pay: federal, state, and local income; Social Security; and Medicare. You can expect the amount deducted to be 15 percent or more of your pay.

Many employers offer direct deposit in which an employee's income goes directly to his or her bank account. It's very convenient: You do not have to cash a check, and your bank may offer free checking when you have direct deposit.

Your employer may offer other benefits to you, especially if you are a full-time employee (that is, you work over a certain number of hours per week). Those benefits most likely will be something other than money, such as vacation or sick days. If your employer offers you an opportunity to have various kinds of insurance, you probably will have to pay a portion of the cost, which will be taken from your paycheck.

Create a Plan for Spending Your Income

If your paycheck includes a pay stub, find a safe place to keep it. You may need to refer to the stubs to monitor changes in your pay, taxes, the number of vacation or sick days you have available, and so on. You can also use the pay stubs to compare the pay offered by other employers.

As soon as you receive your first paycheck, prepare a spending plan, and plan to spend as little as possible of your first few paychecks for at least two reasons:

- Most new jobs have a 90-day probationary period in which the employer can fire you if you do not meet the expectations.
- You may quickly find that you do not like the work and may choose to find a different job.

Complete the following worksheet to record your spending plan.

YOUR SPENDING PLAN

How much do you spend in a month? In the following worksheet, keep track of your monthly expenses.

Income	Amount
Monthly income from job	$_____
Additional income	_____
Total Income	_____

Expense	Amount
Food	$_____
Housing	_____
Transportation	_____
Utilities	_____
Entertainment	_____
Savings	_____
Other:_____	_____
_____	_____
_____	_____
Total Expenses	_____

© JIST Works. Duplication Prohibited.

STEP 3: Develop Your People Skills

Don't underestimate the importance of getting to know the people in your workplace. Not getting along is one of the main reasons for being unhappy with a job and one of the top reasons people are fired. Use the following worksheet to rate how you fit in with the people in your work environment.

THE PEOPLE IN YOUR WORKPLACE

Record the number of people in your workplace who have the following characteristics:

Characteristic	Group	Number of Employees
Age Range	Younger than 16	_____
	16–18 years old	_____
	19–21 years old	_____
	22–24 years old	_____
	25–34 years old	_____
	35–44 years old	_____
	45–54 years old	_____
	55–64 years old	_____
	65 and older	_____
Age Compared to Yours	Younger than you are	_____
	Your own age	_____
	Older than you are	_____
Gender	Female	_____
	Male	_____
Culture	African-American	_____
	Asian	_____
	Hispanic	_____

Characteristic	Group	Number of Employees
	Native American	_____
	Caucasion	_____
Education	High school graduates	_____
	Trade school graduates	_____
	College graduates	_____
Education Compared to Yours	Less educated than you are	_____
	As educated as you are	_____
	More educated than you are	_____
Number of People You Work with Daily	Others from your department	_____
	Customers	_____
	Employees from other departments	_____
	Managers/Supervisors	_____
	Customers	_____

On an average day, which group do you have the most contact with?

With very few exceptions, your workplace will require you to deal with other people, and most of your dealings will be with your boss and your co-workers. Making sure you get along with these people is a critical factor in your job success.

Respect Your Supervisor

First, let's take a look at your relationship with your supervisor. This person has the responsibility to make sure that you know what to do, how to do it, and when to do it. Some supervisors are great managers who can inspire, motivate, and lead a team with mutual respect. Some are simply bad managers. Most fall somewhere in the middle. No matter what your supervisor is like, you must find a way to get along and be effective with the style of management the supervisor uses.

Ten Rules for Getting Along with Your Supervisor

Whatever your supervisor's style, you are the one who must adapt. U.S. Air Force Colonel Phillip Meilinger offered some good advice in his article "Ten Rules of Good Followership" in *Military Review:*

1. Don't blame the boss.
2. Do your homework.
3. Don't fight the boss.
4. Be willing to implement the suggestions you make.
5. Use initiative.
6. Keep the boss informed.
7. Accept responsibility.
8. Fix problems as they occur.
9. Tell the truth and don't quibble.
10. Put in an honest day's work.

Take Direction with an Open Mind

As you learn your job, your supervisor and other co-workers will play important roles in your training. You may want to do things differently than the way they are training you. You may not like being told you are doing something the wrong way. Your first instinct may be to snap at the person giving you directions.

Before you get angry or defensive, find out why a specific process has been designed the way it is. Maybe you'll change your mind about how you do something. Or, if you are calm and polite during the training, you may later be given an opportunity to teach your new co-workers a better way to do it.

Always remember that people who help or train you are giving you the gift of their time and experience. Accept that gift with respect, and you will likely gain the respect of your supervisor and co-workers in return.

Be a Team Player

When you are working, you are part of a team. You may work with several other people who have the same responsibilities you have, or you may be the only one who has them. Either way, you are still part of a team that must work well together for the organization to be successful.

Let's say that you work on the last shift as one of several chef assistants in a fine restaurant. The chef and the assistants who work with you will be much more productive and happier if you complete your share of the work as quickly, carefully, and accurately as you can. The assistants who work different shifts will appreciate having the foods prepared appropriately and the equipment clean and ready for them. You may feel that others will not notice what goes on behind the closed kitchen doors, but the customers will notice whether the food is prepared properly. The serving staff will notice when the customers are pleased. The success of the entire restaurant depends on every employee working together as a team.

If you work alone in a position, you are still part of a team. Here is an example: You are the only receptionist for a medical office with several doctors. Each doctor has a medical assistant. Even though you are the only receptionist, you are part of the medical team. You are responsible for getting information to the right people at the right time. If you do not work well with the others, the negativity may spill over to the patients, visiting sales people, maintenance staff, and others.

Answer the questions in the following worksheet to see whether you are a team player.

Your Teamwork Skills

For each of the following questions, check "Yes" or "No."

Do You	Yes	No
1. Refuse to take part in workplace social activities?	❏	❏
2. Share secrets others have told in confidence?	❏	❏
3. Always try to smile and be friendly?	❏	❏
4. Leave your work area a mess because that's how you like it?	❏	❏
5. Listen when others talk without interrupting them?	❏	❏
6. Offer to take on extra work when a co-worker gets called away by a family emergency?	❏	❏
7. Offer a ride when someone is having car trouble?	❏	❏
8. Tell the supervisor when someone has helped you?	❏	❏
9. Talk constantly about how things were at another job?	❏	❏
10. Arrive at work on time so that others don't have to cover for you?	❏	❏
11. Frequently try to sell something to co-workers?	❏	❏
12. Work as carefully, efficiently, and cheerfully as you can?	❏	❏
13. Tell off-color jokes?	❏	❏

(continued)

(continued)

14. Invite co-workers to lunch? ❏ ❏

15. Brag about good performance reviews and raises you receive? ❏ ❏

List any areas you know you need to change.

_____

_____

_____

Beside each area you listed, write the date by which you want to change it.

Pay Attention to How You Communicate with Others

In a worksheet in Step 2, you looked at how you fit in with your co-workers. Regardless of age, race, gender, and education, you can take steps to work effectively with the people around you. Recognize where the differences are, think about how you communicate with your co-workers, and get to know them to help you move beyond the differences.

For example, think about how you greet other people. If you are too informal or loud, some co-workers may think you are disrespectful or inappropriate. If you never respond to others when they greet you, they may think that you are mad or disagreeable.

Proper Introductions. The right way to make an introduction between two people is to introduce a lower-ranking person to a higher-ranking person. For example, if your boss is Ms. Jones and you are introducing the administrative assistant John Smith to her, the correct introduction would be, "Ms. Jones, I'd like you to meet John Smith."

Pay attention to other people's reactions to you. If you smile and a co-worker smiles back and responds warmly, you're fine. If the co-worker says very little to you and walks away quickly when you approach, you may have created a conflict that you need to resolve—especially if the behavior continues over a few days. In the next section, you will read about resolving conflicts.

When communicating with others, remember that you cannot read their minds. Don't assume that loudness or quietness mean that people are angry. People from some other cultural groups may have grown up shouting to get their point across or believing that they need to be very quiet. If you are in doubt about what co-workers are thinking or feeling, wait for an appropriate time and then ask politely and kindly how they are doing. Courtesy and kindness are acceptable in any culture.

Resolve Conflicts Quickly

The best thing to do when you are involved in a conflict is to talk to the person directly. Find a time and a place when it's just the two of you. Keep your conversation focused on the positive side. For instance, don't accuse your co-worker or say something like, "Hey, you need to get over yourself. Lighten up and be cool."

>
> **Don't be part of the problem.** According to the research completed by Christine Porath, an assistant professor in the Marshall School of Business at the University of Southern California, one of eight employees who feels disrespected in a workplace eventually leaves it. Don't be the reason your co-workers are unhappy!

Instead, say something more positive. Even apologize first, if necessary, saying something like this: "Excuse me. I get the feeling that somehow I've offended you by something I said or did. I really want us to work well together, and I would like to know if I've done something wrong. I want to make it right."

If you calmly begin the conversation as soon as you sense a problem, you can resolve it quickly and move on. Plus, you'll establish a greater bond of trust with that co-worker. And that makes for a much happier, more productive team.

Respect Others by Listening to Them

Because our minds can absorb information much faster than people speak, we must make an effort to listen without letting our mind drift to other things—such as what to say next. The key to paying attention during a conversation is *active listening*. Active listening can be defined as simply listening with a purpose.

Read these four traits of active listening and then check yourself to see how often you practice them:

1. Focus on the person who is talking rather than on yourself.

2. Listen without trying to protect yourself from being hurt by the other person's words, beliefs, or attitudes.

3. Listen to the other's feelings, opinions, or experiences and don't assume that they are the same as yours. Put yourself in the other person's place and try to imagine what is behind that person's thoughts.

> **Quip**
> According to the article "Active Listening: Hear What People Are Really Saying" by Kellie Fowler at www.mindtools.com, people speak at a rate of 100 to 175 words per minute, but they can listen intelligently at a rate of 600 to 800 words per minute.

4. Listen to understand—not to criticize, change, or agree with the other person.

Showing others you care about what they say is an important part of respect. Following are ten specific skills that indicate that you are listening. You might need some practice, but learning these skills will help you at work—and with friends and family.

TEN SKILLS FOR ACTIVE LISTENING*

Skill	How You Can Show It
Acknowledging	Looking at people as they speak.
Restating	Repeating what others say, but using your own words.
Reflecting	Using facial expressions or words such as "You look happy" that let others know you are paying attention to their feelings and experiences.
Interpreting	Telling others how their feelings, desires, or meanings are coming across to you, as in "I'm sensing that you are unhappy."
Summarizing	Stating the main points of what has been discussed.
Probing	Asking questions in a caring way so that you can clear up confusions, as in "Can you tell me what I said that hurt your feelings?"
Giving feedback	Sharing how you react to others' words or feelings, as in "I'm not sure I understand," or "Your words make me really happy."
Supporting them.	In your own way, showing others that you care about
Checking perceptions	Asking others whether you are understanding what they are saying.
Being quiet	Giving others time to think and talk without interruptions.

*Adapted from "Communication" by Marisue Pickering, in EXPLORATIONS, A Journal of Research of the University of Maine, Vol. 3, No. 1, Fall 1986, pp 16–19.

Be a Team Builder

Active listening is just one way to show your respect for co-workers. There are other simple things you can do, too. Look back at Step 1, and work on eliminating the bad habits that can annoy others or prevent them from doing their jobs.

Another simple gesture is to give credit where it's due. When someone helps you, say "thank you" and make sure to tell the manager how much you appreciated the help. When someone tries to give you credit for another person's ideas, speak up and identify the person responsible for the ideas. Follow your company's policy for formal recognition when somebody helps you.

Finally, share what you have learned with others if they are open to your input, and ask for help when you need it. See others in the organization and yourself as part of a team working together for the success of the organization, not as competitors.

Respect Others' Work Areas

Respect others by leaving their work areas and personal property alone. Unless you ask permission, don't take things that don't belong to you. Don't move things around in another person's office. Put papers in designated "in" boxes. Leave a note with any items you leave in someone else's work space to let them know what the item is, what action needs to be taken with it, and who left it. Such simple courtesies can have big pay-offs for your career.

Learn How to Handle Difficult Co-workers

Some supervisors or co-workers can be difficult to work with. This can create unnecessary stress in the workplace. Be aware when someone is affecting your performance on the job by

- Teasing that embarrasses you
- Inappropriately shifting work responsibilities to you
- Threatening you with physical harm
- Subjecting you to sexual or other comments or behaviors that offend you

What should you do if you believe that you are the brunt of inappropriate behavior? The following list can help you:

- No one should have to accept on-the-job harassment. There are laws designed to protect you, and most organizations require that you immediately report such behavior internally. If you don't have an employee handbook or it doesn't mention harassment, ask in advance for the procedure to follow in reporting harassment or intimidation of any kind. If you feel physically threatened, you should consider leaving the workplace and reporting the behavior once you are safe.

- For less threatening situations, you can discuss the situation with a trusted co-worker or friend to help you determine whether you are correct in your interpretation or are being too sensitive.

- If you are not afraid for your physical safety, calmly and politely discuss the situation with the person who is being difficult. He or she may just be insensitive and not understand the impact of the behavior.

- If the difficulty does not stop, follow the reporting procedure in your employee manual or report it to your immediate supervisor. If your organization does not correct the problem, you may consider contacting the Equal Employment Opportunity Commission at info@ask.eeoc.gov. You need to include your city, state, and ZIP code so that your e-mail will be sent to the appropriate office.

- After you have reported the problem, continue to be polite, do your job well, strengthen your relationships with other co-workers (but do not gossip or complain about the difficulty), and believe in yourself. You deserve respect, especially self-respect in difficult times.

Think About the Customer

Building people skills starts by thinking about your co-workers and yourself, but it also includes focusing on the people who come in contact with your organization. You have to put yourself in your customer's shoes. If you were the customer, how would you want to be treated?

When you can serve customers in a way that leads to their total satisfaction, you create powerful impressions of yourself and of your employer. Based on those impressions, customers decide whether to return and what to say to other potential customers about you. This affects the success of your organization—and your reputation.

Take a moment to complete the following worksheet. Decide whether you have the customer focus you need to succeed.

THE DEFINITION OF GOOD CUSTOMER SERVICE

Write your answers to the following questions. They will help you focus on your personal definition of good customer service.

1. Describe a personal experience you had when you received really good customer service. _____
   _____
   _____

2. Describe a personal experience you had when you received really bad customer service. _____

_____

_____

Place a checkmark under the Yes if you consider the following actions to be good customer service or under No if you consider them to be poor customer service.

Actions	Yes	No
Smiling at customers	❏	❏
Greeting customers in a warm, friendly voice	❏	❏
Letting the phone ring a few times before you answer it	❏	❏
Letting a customer look for something on his/her own	❏	❏
Returning customer phone calls promptly	❏	❏
Promising to look into a problem you can't solve	❏	❏
Taking personal phone calls while customers are waiting	❏	❏
Walking away from an angry customer	❏	❏
Listening closely to what a customer says	❏	❏

Write your definition of good customer service.

_____

_____

You can use active listening skills to help you look at your organization, co-workers, and yourself through the customers' eyes.

You may have learned the Golden Rule, "Do unto others as you would have do unto you," but with customers, the rule is that you don't think of what *you* want but what *customers* want.

What if the customer is angry? If you calmly talk with the customer, you normally can quickly resolve the conflict. If a customer will not calm down, you may need to turn to your manager for help. Know your organization's policy for handling a customer problem before it occurs.

STEP 4: Make the Right Choices

Every single day, you have to make decisions about the kind of employee you will be. You have to choose between right and wrong. The choices you make determine the reputation you will have.

Be Honest

Dishonesty is one of the reasons why employees are fired. Lying on an application or resume is grounds for dismissal. Taking an employer's property can also result in someone's being fired. Those are obvious wrongs and may be unthinkable to you.

But there are small ways of being dishonest that can creep up on us all. Is it lying to report that you have completed more work than you have? Is it stealing to take a handful of the paperclips or packages of sweetener from the office supply when you're running low on them at home? It's the little things that no one may catch you doing that can lead to your being comfortable with wrongs you once would never have considered doing.

Report to Work When Scheduled

The "Out of the Office 2005" survey by CareerBuilder.com showed that during the past year 43% of Americans called in sick when they really weren't. The reasons they gave for missing work included a desire to relax (23%), they just didn't feel like going to work (16%), or they had a doctor's appointment (16%) or household or personal errands (9%).

Think about the effect your absence has. When you aren't at work, who has to do your work? Will your co-workers have to do more than their share to cover for you? Will someone else be called in from a planned day off to cover for you? Will customers have to wait longer for service? Will the work just pile up and be worse when you return?

> **Nobody wins when you choose to miss work unexpectedly—including you.**

When you accept a new job, you are making a promise to be there. And when you're there, you're making a promise to do your work. Sometimes all it takes is more careful planning on your part to make sure that you can be at your job when you are supposed to be. Use your sick days for when you really are ill, and plan ahead to show up for work when you are scheduled. Use the worksheet on the next page to map out your personal weekly schedule.

Your Weekly Schedule

Use this worksheet to plan your weekly schedule. List both the activity and the time it will require to complete it. Write in the activities you *want* to do, as well as those you *must* do.

Weekly Appointments

Day	Work	School	Other
Sunday			
Monday			
Tuesday			

(continued)

(continued)

Day	Work	School	Other
Wednesday			
Thursday			
Friday			
Saturday			

Manage Your Time Well While on the Job

One of the easiest ways to upset your workplace is constant interruption from your family and friends. Think about the time you spend at work on your personal issues. How many times a day do you get calls or e-mail from your friends? Your spouse? Your children? Whether you take the call or e-mail on your cell phone or e-mail system, these interruptions pull you away from what you are being paid to do. If they are for the safety and security of your family, try to follow these guidelines:

- Schedule the contacts during your regular break times or lunch hours.
- Keep the contacts short.
- Keep other co-workers from hearing your personal calls or seeing your e-mail.
- Put your personal call on hold while you wait on customers—or offer to call back when customers are gone.
- Turn your cell phone on vibrate or very low volume to keep the ring from bothering others.
- Never discuss anything intimate—sex, health, money, legal issues—in a way that others can hear you.

Handle Childcare and Other Personal Duties the Right Way

Keeping all personal business away from work can be difficult. From time to time, you may need to have your car repaired, arrange for someone to fix an appliance at home, or handle a variety of childcare responsibilities. Life happens, and work is not your only responsibility. Your challenge is to handle as many of these other duties as possible outside of your job. Doing so will require planning like that in the preceding weekly schedule worksheet.

Here is an example: If you have children, you may need to have a backup plan in place for their care. When your regular childcare falls through and you have a backup plan, you can quickly make the change—without missing work. The backup plan will ease your mind and prevent problems on the job.

If you have a family, you will want to look at your family schedule at the beginning of each week. Think ahead. Can you schedule other appointments on your days off? If not, can you move those appointments to a lunch hour? Can a spouse, friend, or older child take care of something for you? Can you let your boss and co-workers know in advance that you must miss work? If you can keep your work life and your personal life separated, you will increase your chance for success on the job.

Don't Abuse the Technology at Your Fingertips

It's so easy to abuse technology. The phone is right there. The computer is right there. You're not hurting anyone by using them for personal contact. Right? Wrong.

If you have access to a phone and a computer, that access is for business reasons. The costs for that access are being paid by an employer who expects results. If you've got a phone line tied up to talk about last night's episode of your favorite TV show, a customer can't get through to place an order. If your e-mail box is full of jokes and spam, the risk of bringing a virus into your business network goes up dramatically and the space on the server goes down. If you're surfing the Internet for a great deal on a new car, your work is sitting unfinished. All these activities are a form of theft because you are being paid to work, not to engage in personal activities. Take a moment to read The *Do*s and *Don't*s of Using Technology sidebar.

The *Do*s and *Don't*s of Using Technology

Do

- Protect your computer password.
- Use the computer only as you have been trained to do.
- Route computer messages to only the people who need them.
- Follow procedures to avoid introducing viruses to the internal computer network.
- Clean out your e-mail box regularly.
- Follow all established policies for doing online research.
- Report any security issues immediately.
- Limit personal phone calls while at work (incoming and outgoing).
- Set your phone's ringer volume so it won't disrupt co-workers.
- Keep your voice mail box cleared to accept incoming messages.

Don't

- Use your work e-mail to send jokes.
- Spend work time surfing the Internet for pleasure.
- Use e-mail to gripe about others.
- Visit any inappropriate Internet sites.

- Access information that does not apply to your job.
- Leave customers waiting while you take a personal phone call.
- Conduct intimate phone calls or fights in open work areas.
- Play voice mail messages on the speaker phone.

Manage Yourself

Making the right choices comes down to one thing: you. You are the one who must decide every day how you will act. Will you choose right? Will you choose wrong? Use the following worksheet to rate how you perform.

YOUR SELF-MANAGEMENT SKILLS

For each statement below, check Yes or No. Are there areas you need to change?

Do You	Yes	No
1. Come to work every day as scheduled?	❑	❑
2. Know what to do when you get to your work area?	❑	❑
3. Ask too many questions about day-to-day work?	❑	❑
4. Remember to attend meetings and get there on time?	❑	❑
5. Finish your work on time?	❑	❑
6. Follow the rules and processes for your job?	❑	❑
7. Know safety and emergency policies?	❑	❑
8. Work out disagreements with co-workers directly?	❑	❑
9. Keep your promises?	❑	❑
10. Admit when you are wrong?	❑	❑
11. Show respect for your supervisor and your co-workers?	❑	❑
12. Keep your work area and tools organized?	❑	❑
13. Try to learn new things to help yourself and your co-workers?	❑	❑
14. Do your work right the first time?	❑	❑
15. Work to solve problems that come up unexpectedly?	❑	❑

STEP 5: Build on Your Reputation

Good reputations are not given; they are earned. They are the payoff for making good choices. You are the one who creates your reputation.

Every choice you make reflects back on you. When you make good choices, people notice. They learn that they can rely on you—or not. They learn to expect good things when you're around—or not. They decide that they want to reward you—or not.

Give a Little to Gain Much More

You can build on your reputation by making a few simple additions to what is typically expected of you. Arrive at work a little early. You can use the time to discuss the day's work with your co-workers from a previous shift. Or you can turn on equipment, unlock doors, organize your workplace, put on your uniform, and check phone or e-mail messages before your shift starts.

At the end of your scheduled work time, stay a few minutes. Use this time to turn job information over to those working after you. Or offer to help your work team complete a big project. Or finish taking care of a customer. Also, straighten up your work area so you'll be ready to begin working when you return. You might sacrifice a few minutes of your personal time, but you will definitely show those around you that doing a good job is important to you.

TASKS THAT BUILD YOUR REPUTATION

Place a checkmark in front of those tasks you are willing to do to build on your reputation.

- ❏ Arrive a few minutes early.
- ❏ Turn on equipment.
- ❏ Give project or work updates to those on your team.
- ❏ Share the responsibility of organizing social events.
- ❏ Straighten a central work area.
- ❏ Help decorate for the holidays.
- ❏ Stay a few minutes late to finish an important project.

Others:

_____
_____
_____

Think Like a Supervisor

To build on your reputation, you must progress from thinking only about yourself to thinking like a supervisor. Complete the worksheet below to identify whether you are meeting what you would expect of someone under your supervision.

Your Expectations as a Supervisor

Place a checkmark in front of those expectations you know you would have if you were the supervisor.

- ❏ Have an ability to analyze
- ❏ Model dependability
- ❏ Be a team player
- ❏ Show flexibility
- ❏ Communicate effectively
- ❏ Practice honesty
- ❏ Lead and manage others
- ❏ Show openness to new ideas
- ❏ Manage priorities
- ❏ Keep a positive attitude
- ❏ Operate the computer
- ❏ Show professionalism
- ❏ Plan and organize work
- ❏ Have self-confidence
- ❏ Prioritize customer service
- ❏ Be willing to learn
- ❏ Solve problems
- ❏ Show dedication to the job
- ❏ Work well with others
- ❏ Work without supervision

Following are some tips for figuring out whether you need to work on any of the preceding skills.

- Think about how you act every day at work.
- Look closely at how you do your job and ask yourself whether there is more you could learn in order to do your job better.
- Think about whether there are skills you need or want to improve. Is there anything you need to change?
- Think about ways your work connects to the work of other people or other departments.
- Think about what you want to do next. Decide how your current job can help you get ready for the next step.
- Look for gaps in your training or experience that need to be filled. What actions do you need to take?

- Ask for others to give you feedback on how you're doing.
- Identify people you think are doing a good job and hang out with them. Figure out what makes them different from those who are less successful. Are they different from you?

Keep On Learning

Your workplace may have formal learning opportunities, but those will help you only if you make the move. You have to have the attitude that learning is the right thing do. Then you have to go after those opportunities yourself.

Work with your boss and your human resource department to find ways you can improve your skills. Whether you just want to be better in your current position or you're looking for a promotion, start with improving your skills.

Use the following worksheet to identify training resources you might use.

ADDITIONAL LEARNING RESOURCES AVAILABLE TO YOU

Place a checkmark in front of the learning resources that are available to you for learning additional skills.

- ❏ Personal counseling
- ❏ Job shadowing program
- ❏ Formal mentoring program
- ❏ Trade magazines
- ❏ Trade association or union resources
- ❏ Trade shows, conferences, and workshops
- ❏ Financial assistance for schooling

Others:

_____

_____

_____

Thinking like a supervisor and continuing to learn can be protections against being laid off (also referred to as downsized or fired). The more valuable you are to your employer, the more reluctant that employer will be to lose you as an employee.

STEP 6: Create a Career Plan

You may just be starting out in a new job, but you already need to be thinking about the future. Dream about where this job can lead you. Plan how you can grow in your career from this point to the next. Prepare yourself so that you'll be ready when opportunity knocks.

Notice that we are shifting from using the word *job* exclusively to using the word *career* from time to time. A *job* is the work you do to earn money; a *career* is the direction you take with your life—your paid and unpaid work, your lifelong education, and the life roles you accept (parent, friend, employee, and so on).

Create SMART Goals

To have a plan that will move your career forward, you need SMART goals. They are goals that are

S = Specific

M = Measurable

A = Achievable

R = Realistic

T = Time-Bound

Writing a goal that is *specific* means that you include details when you are writing it. For example, know what job title you want to have in the future. Describe what your work area looks like. Think about where you'll be working. Write a description of the type of activities you'll be doing.

Having a *measurable* goal means you will be able to know when you've reached your goal. Reaching a goal should mean that you make a change from where you start to where you finish. A goal can be measured by the amount of money you make or number of people you manage. It could be the number of items you make or sell or miles you travel.

An *achievable* goal is one that is possible. It may not be reasonable to set a goal to double your annual pay next week, for example, but that goal *is* possible if you just change your time frame to a few years.

Realistic means that the goal must be practical. Choose a goal that you will find interesting and enjoyable, not one that you resist and try to avoid. If you know that you need to lose weight to become a fire fighter, but you hate dieting, don't set a dieting goal; choose another way of losing weight, such as taking an hour-long bike ride or walking three times a week so that your weight drops off gradually and you can qualify for a fire fighter position within a year.

A *time-bound* goal is one that has a date on it. Set the number of hours, days, weeks, months, or years it will take you to reach the goal. Include some milestone dates between now and your end goal. For example, you may want to make it your goal to complete an Accounting class by May of next year so that you can enroll in a management training program next July and start an internship next September. All these goals are stepping stones to the ultimate goal of having a management-level job within the next 18 months.

You may not have noticed, but you've practiced making SMART goals in several earlier worksheets in this booklet.

Write Your Plan

Take a few minutes to think about your own career goals. Use the worksheet that follows to write them down. In the second part of the worksheet, write down any gaps you have in your skills or training. Emphasize the specific actions you need to take to make your goals come true.

YOUR PERSONAL GOALS

Complete each of the following steps to create your own personal goals.

1. Think about what you want to achieve in your career. Write a SMART goal for your career. _____

2. Now think about the skills you will need to reach that goal. What action(s) can you take to reach it? _____

3. By what date do you plan to reach that goal? _____

4. Write a second goal for your career. _____

5. Think about the skills you will need to reach that goal. What action(s) can you take to reach it? _____
_____
_____
_____

6. By what date do you plan to reach that goal? _____

7. Write a third goal for your career. _____
_____

8. Think about the skills you will need to reach that goal. What action(s) can you take to reach it? _____
_____
_____
_____

9. By what date do you plan to reach that goal? _____

Keep Your Plan Updated

Your career plan should not collect dust on a shelf. After you have it, keep working on it and keep notes on your progress in a separate notebook, file, or career portfolio. Add to the education section in your resume when you complete a training class. Record your volunteer activities. Update your job objective every time you reach a milestone, such as getting a raise or a new work assignment.

These records will be useful when you ask for a promotion or an increase in pay. If you need to change jobs for some reason, they will also allow you to quickly update your resume and career plan.

Keep Your Basic Job Search Tools Updated

Even if you think you will stay on your job for a long time, there are reasons to keep your resume and other job search tools up to date. One reason is that layoffs can sometimes happen suddenly due to mergers, downsizing, or other reasons beyond your control. Or you may decide to look for another job for a variety of reasons. Most importantly, updating your job search tools on a regular basis will help you keep your career goals in focus.

Update Your JIST Card®

A JIST Card® is a type of mini-resume. It is very small, but packed with information that is most important to an employer. Look at the sample cards on page 39. They are JIST Cards, and they get results. Computer printed or even neatly written on 3-by-5–inch cards, JIST Cards include the essential information employers want to know:

- **Name.** Use your name as it is spoken. Avoid nicknames.

- **Phone number.** People will most likely contact you by phone or e-mail. If you cannot answer your home phone during the day (or if you don't have a phone), ask a reliable friend or relative to take messages. Another option is to get voice-mail or an answering machine. Just make sure your message sounds professional. Many JIST Cards include a second phone number to increase the chance of others reaching you. This may be a pager number, a cell phone number, or some other alternative phone number.

- **E-mail address.** Include your e-mail address if you have one. Keep in mind that free e-mail accounts are available through a variety of sources. If you don't have a computer, you can use an Internet connection at a library to access your account.

- **Position or job objective.** If your job objective is too specific, it will limit the jobs for which you may be considered. Instead, use a job objective that allows you to be considered for more positions but is not too general.

- **Skills.** Skills can be reflected in several ways:
  - **Education and experience.** Take credit for everything you've done. Everything can count, including education, training, paid employment, related volunteer work, hobbies, and other informal experience. Add up the total amount of time you have spent gaining this experience.
  - **Job-related skills and results.** Mention the skills you can do specific to the job, such as using special tools or computers. Emphasize your accomplishments and, whenever possible, use numbers (such as percentage of sales or profits increased, number of units produced, and so on) in describing them.
  - **Transferable skills.** Mention ones that are important to the job and that you do well. Use examples where possible.
  - **Self-management skills.** Include at least three of your strongest self-management skills.
  - **Special conditions.** This is an optional section. Use it to list special advantages you offer that don't fit elsewhere.

Sample JIST Cards

Ricardo Nunez

Position: General Office/Clerical

Message: (512) 232-9213

More than two years of work experience plus one year of training in office practices. Type 55 wpm, trained in word processing, post general ledger, have good interpersonal skills, and get along with most people. Can meet deadlines and handle pressure well.

Willing to work any hours.

Organized, honest, reliable, and hardworking.

Rebecca Stowell **Home: (602) 253-9678**
  Message: (602) 257-6643
  E-mail: RSS@email.cmm

Objective: Electronics installation, maintenance, and sales

Four years of work experience plus a two-year A.S. degree in Electronics Engineering Technology. Managed a $360,000/year business while going to school full time, with grades in the top 25%. Familiar with all major electronic diagnostic and repair equipment. Hands-on experience with medical, consumer, communication, and industrial electronics equipment and applications. Good problem-solving and communication skills. Customer service oriented.

Willing to do what it takes to get the job done.

Self-motivated, dependable, learn quickly.

You can easily create JIST Cards on a computer and print them on card stock you can buy at any office supply store. Or have a few hundred printed cheaply at a local quick-print shop. While JIST Cards are often done as 3-by-5 cards, they can be printed in any size or format. Make sure that you keep your JIST Card up to date.

Keep Your Resume Current

Maintaining your resume is important even when you are totally satisfied with your current job. You never know when you may need to apply for a promotion or seek employment with another organization.

Many resumes use a chronological format that lists the most recent experience first, followed by each previous job. This arrangement works fine for someone with work experience in several similar jobs, but not as well for those with limited experience or for career changers.

Look at the resumes on pages 41 and 42. Jendayi Jones' resume uses the chronological approach. Catalina Garcia's skills resume emphasizes her most important skills, supported by specific examples of how she has used them. This type of resume allows her to use any part of her life history to support her ability to do the job she wants.

Follow these tips as you update your resume:

- **Name.** Use your formal name rather than a nickname if it sounds more professional.

- **Address and contact information.** Avoid abbreviations in your address and include your ZIP code and your area code in your phone number. Give alternative ways to reach you, such as a cell phone and e-mail address.

- **Job objective.** You should almost always have one, even if it is general.

- **Education and training.** Include any training or education you've had that supports your job objective (even if you did not finish a formal degree or program).

- **Previous experience.** Include the employer name, job title, dates employed, and responsibilities—but emphasize specific skills, results, accomplishments, and superior performance.

- **Promotions.** You can list a promotion to a more responsible job as a separate job.

- **Personal data.** Do not include details such as height, weight, and marital status or a photo. Current laws do not allow an employer to base hiring decisions on these points.

- **References.** Make sure that each person will make nice comments about you, and then list your references on a separate page to give to employers who ask.

Sample Chronological Resume

Jendayi Jones

115 South Hawthorne Avenue
Chicago, Illinois 66204

jj@earthlink.net
(312) 653-9217

Adds lots of details to reinforce skills throughout.

JOB OBJECTIVE

Provides more details here.

Seeking a position requiring excellent business management expertise in an office environment. Position should require a variety of skills, including office management, word processing, and spreadsheet and database application use.

EDUCATION AND TRAINING

Acme Business College, Lincoln, IL
Completed one-year program in Professional Office Management. Achieved GPA in top 30% of class. Courses included word processing, accounting theory and systems, advanced spreadsheet and database applications, graphics design, time management, and supervision.

John Adams High School, South Bend, IN
Graduated with emphasis on business courses. Earned excellent grades in all business topics and won top award for word-processing speed and accuracy.

Other: Continuing-education programs at own expense, including business communications, customer relations, computer applications, and sales techniques.

EXPERIENCE

Uses numbers to reinforce results.

2003–present—**Claims Processor, Blue Spear Insurance Company,** Wilmette, IL. Process 50 complex medical insurance claims per day, almost 20% above department average. Created a spreadsheet report process that decreased department labor costs by more than $30,000 a year. Received two merit raises for performance.

2002–2003—**Returned to business school to gain advanced office skills.**

1999–2002—**Finance Specialist (E4), U.S. Army.** Systematically processed more than 200 invoices per day from commercial vendors. Trained and supervised eight employees. Devised internal system allowing 15% increase in invoices processed with a decrease in personnel. Managed department with a budget equivalent of more than $350,000 a year. Honorable discharge.

1998–1999—**Sales Associate promoted to Assistant Manager, Sandy's Boutique,** Wilmette, IL. Made direct sales and supervised four employees. Managed daily cash balances and deposits, made purchasing and inventory decisions, and handled all management functions during owner's absence. Sales increased 26% and profits doubled during tenure.

1996–1998—**Held various part-time and summer jobs through high school while maintaining GPA 3.0/4.0.** Earned enough to pay all personal expenses, including car insurance. Learned to deal with customers, meet deadlines, work hard, and handle multiple priorities.

STRENGTHS AND SKILLS

Reliable, with strong work ethic. Excellent interpersonal, written, and oral communication and math skills. Accept supervision well, effectively supervise others, and work well as a team member. General ledger, accounts payable, and accounts receivable expertise. Proficient in Microsoft Word, Excel, and Outlook; WordPerfect.

The Skills Resume for Those with Limited Work Experience

In this skills resume, each skill directly supports the job objective of this recent high school graduate with very limited work experience.

Catalina A. Garcia
2340 N. Delaware Street · Denver, Colorado 81613
Home: (413) 643-2173 (Leave Message)
Cell phone: (413) 345-2189
E-mail: cagarcia@net.net

Position Desired

Office assistant in a fast-paced business

Note her key skills.

Support for her key skills comes from her activities: school, clubs, and volunteer work.

Skills and Abilities

Communications — Excellent written and verbal presentation skills. Use proper grammar and have a good speaking voice.

Interpersonal — Able to get along well with all types of people. Accept supervision. Received positive evaluation from previous supervisors.

Flexible — Willing to try new things and am interested in improving efficiency on assigned tasks.

Notice the emphasis on adaptive skills.

Attention to Detail — Maintained confidential student records accurately and efficiently. Uploaded 500 student records in one day without errors.

Hard Working — Worked 30 hours per week throughout high school and maintained above-average grades.

She makes good use of numbers.

This statement is very strong.

Student Contact — Cordially dealt with as many as 150 students a day in Dean's office.

Dependable — Never absent or tardy in four years.

Awards — English Department Student of the Year, April 20XX
20XX Outstanding Student Newspaper, Newspaper Association of America

Education

Denver North High School. Took advanced English and communication classes. Member of student newspaper staff and FCCLA for four years. Graduated in top 30% of class.

Other

Girls' basketball team for four years. This taught me discipline, teamwork, how to follow instructions, and hard work. I am ambitious, outgoing, reliable, and willing to work.

Catalina's resume makes it clear that she is talented and hard working.

When you have maintained an updated version of your resume, you are ready for any changes that affect your employment. You can quickly and easily submit the updated resume to your supervisor, the supervisor of another department, or perhaps even a different employer.

Always make sure that your resume meets the following standards:

- **It is error-free.** One spelling or grammar error will create a negative impressionist (see what we mean?). Get someone else to review your final draft for any errors. Then review it again because these rascals have a way of slipping in.

- **It looks good.** Poor copy quality, cheap paper, bad type quality, or anything else that creates a poor appearance will turn off employers to even the best resume content. Get professional help with design and printing if necessary. Many professional resume writers and even print shops offer writing and desktop design services if you need help.

- **It is brief and relevant.** Many good resumes fit on one page, and few justify more than two. Include only the most important points. Use short sentences and action words. If it doesn't relate to and support the job objective, cut it!

- **The information in it is the truth.** Don't overstate your qualifications. If you end up getting a job you can't handle, who does it help? And a lie can result in your being fired later.

- **It is positive.** Emphasize your accomplishments and results. A resume is no place to be too humble or to display your faults.

- **It is specific.** Instead of saying, "I am good with people," say, "I supervised four people in the warehouse and increased productivity by 30 percent." Use numbers whenever possible, such as the number of people served, percent sales increase, or dollars saved.

> **Quip**
>
> **Save your resume electronically.** Each time you change your resume, you will want to save it using a unique filename. We find that it works best to save it with the current date in the filename. That way you know when you last updated it.

STEP 7: Position Yourself to Get Ahead

It doesn't matter at what stage you are in your career. You always need to be working toward the future. Having a clear career plan is a key part of that process. Another critical part is that you put yourself in a position to be promoted or transferred to a better job. You make a plan to get ahead.

Everything you worked through in Steps 1 through 6 gets you to Step 7. Showing a good attitude, knowing your job, being a team player, making good choices, building a good reputation, and defining your goals all play a part in moving you forward. Now let's look at some specific things you can do to ensure future success.

Develop Your Network

Back in Step 3, you learned about introducing yourself to people you didn't know. That is a form of networking. *Networking* is about making connections with other people who can help you in your career. Sometimes they will tell you about new jobs that may interest you. Sometimes they will introduce you to key people you need to know in another department or another organization. Sometimes they will just pass along inside information you need to make a good decision.

Everyone has a network, whether they realize it or not. Your network starts informally with the people in your life. This includes your family, your neighbors, the people in your church or school groups, your current co-workers, the people in your exercise class or softball team, and so on. It's up to you to build your network.

You build your network by getting to know the people you meet. Think about where you work. Think about similar organizations or businesses that interest you. Are there people you admire or respect in those groups? Are there people who have jobs you would like to know more about or even have in the future? If the answer is yes, then you are beginning to shape your network.

Take a few minutes to do the next worksheet. Be sure to think back to your career plan and the SMART goals you wrote. Think about the job you want next in your career. Then write down the names (or titles) of people you want in your network.

YOUR NETWORK CONTACT LIST

List five key people (and their contact information) you want to add to your network.

Name	E-mail Address	Phone Number
1.		
2.		
3.		
4.		
5.		

Reach Out to Work Your Way Up

Now that you've identified who should be in your network, you need to take action. Don't assume that people know they are part of your network—even if they are long-time friends or co-workers. You need to talk to each person individually about being a strong, active part of your personal network.

Before you meet with a network prospect, be prepared. Make sure that you

- Know what you want from the person and why
- Are ready to tell them what you are trying to do in your career—in short, clear statements
- Have a JIST Card, business card, or resume with your phone number and e-mail address on it so they will know how to contact you

When you know you are prepared, begin reaching out to the people you want in your network. Be creative as you make the contacts. Following are a few tips to help you get started:

- Identify a friend or co-worker who knows the person you want in your network and ask to be introduced.
- Send a quick note of congratulations when you hear about something the person has accomplished and mention that you would like to talk about how he or she succeeded.
- Call and ask whether the person would be willing to give you a 30-minute informational interview over a cup of coffee. When you meet, share your resume or your career plan.

- Invite the person to join you at an event or trade meeting you both would find interesting.

- Send an educational article and ask whether the person would be willing to discuss it with you.

Don't Forget to Send Thank-You Notes

Always express your appreciation when someone helps you. Even if the person is a long-time friend or family member, send a formal thank-you note or e-mail. It's a small act that can strengthen your network.

Printed thank-you notes that you mail get a more positive response than e-mailed thank-you notes. You might do both: send an e-mail note and then follow it up with a note you mail. If you do e-mail your thank-you notes, you can adapt some of the tips that follow for use in your e-mail notes.

- **Paper and envelope.** Use good-quality notepaper with matching envelopes. Most stationery stores, card shops, and office-supply stores have these supplies. Avoid cute designs. Notepaper with a simple "Thank You" on the front will do. Off-white and buff colors are good.

- **Typed versus handwritten.** You do not always have to send a formal, typed thank-you letter. Handwritten notes are fine unless your handwriting is illegible or sloppy. A neat, written note can be very effective.

- **Salutation.** Unless you are thanking a friend or relative, don't use first names. Write "Dear Ms. Krenshaw" rather than "Dear Lisa." Include the date.

- **The note.** Keep it short and friendly. This is not the place to write, "I would like to take this time to thank you for...." Remember that the note is just a thank you for what the person did.

- **Your signature.** Use your first and last names. Avoid initials, and make your signature legible.

- **When to send it.** Ideally, you should write your thank-you note immediately after the contact while the details are fresh in your mind and send it within 24 hours of receiving the person's help.

- **Enclosure.** Depending on the situation, enclosing a JIST Card is often a great idea. It's a soft sell that provides your phone number if the person wants to reach you. Make sure your note cards are large enough to hold your JIST Card.

Carefully look at and read the two examples of thank-you notes. Does one look more professional to you than the other?

Sample Thank-You Notes

April 5, XXXX

M. Kijek,

Thanks so much for your willingness to see me next Wednesday at 9 a.m. I know that I am one of many who are interested in working with your organization. I appreciate the opportunity to meet you and learn more about the position.

I've enclosed a JIST Card that presents the basics of my skills for this job and will bring my resume to the interview. Please call me if you have any questions at all.

Sincerely,

Bruce Vernon

Use Networking Cards to Help Organize Follow-Ups

If you use contact management software, you can use it to schedule networking follow-up activities. But the simple paper system we describe here can work very well or can be adapted for managing your networking activities.

Use a simple 3-by-5-inch card to record essential information about each person in your network. Use a 3-by-5-inch card file box to hold the cards. If your networking does not involve a regular schedule, you can file the cards alphabetically by the last name.

However, we've found that staying in touch with good networking contacts can pay off big. You may want to contact each person once a month or more often if that is helpful to you. If you have a definite schedule for contacting members of your network, file your networking cards under the date you want to contact the person. Then follow through by contacting the person on that date.

Here's a sample networking card to give you ideas about creating your own.

Sample Networking Card

```
ORGANIZATION:    Mutual Health Insurance
CONTACT PERSON:  Anna Tomey           PHONE: 317-355-0216
SOURCE OF LEAD:  Aunt Ruth
NOTES: 4/10 Called. Anna on vacation. Call back 4/15. 4/15 Interview set
       4/20 at 1:30. 4/20 Anna showed me around. They use the same computers
       we used in school! (Friendly people.) Sent thank-you note and JIST
       Card, call back 5/1. 5/1 Second interview 5/8 at 9 a.m.!
```

The Giving Side of Networking

Networking doesn't go just one way—it involves giving as well as taking. Be available to the people in your network. If you know that one of your contacts needs help, do what you can to either meet the need or find someone else who can.

Many times people are willing to help others but have difficulty asking for help. Every time you follow up with those in your network, be sure to let them know that you are willing to do whatever you can to help them, too.

Choose a Mentor

Within your network, you may find someone who has lots of knowledge and seems willing to informally teach you what he or she knows. This will probably be someone who has already gone through the process you are in right now—and has succeeded.

You might want to ask this person to be your mentor. A *mentor* is a role model who agrees to work one-on-one with you to help you grow and develop on your own path.

The first quality you want to look for in a mentor is leadership. Review the list of leadership traits below. Think about good leaders you've known, such as coaches, teachers, managers, or team captains. How would you rate them using the Traits of a Good Leader table? And how would you rate yourself?

TRAITS OF A GOOD LEADER*

Trait	How a Leader Demonstrates the Trait
Honesty	Always acts with sincerity and integrity, inspiring trust
Competent	Bases actions on reason and moral principles, never on childlike emotional desires or feelings
Forward-looking	Sets goals and has a vision of the future
Inspiring	Shows endurance in mental, physical, and spiritual stamina, inspiring others to reach for new heights
Intelligent	Reads, studies, and seeks challenging assignments
Fair-minded	Is sensitive to the feelings, values, interests, and well-being of others
Broad-minded	Is open to others and their ideas
Courageous	Displays a confident calmness under stress
Creative	Shows creativity by thinking of new and better goals, ideas, and solutions to problems

*Adapted from the list compiled by the Santa Clara University and the Tom Peters Group

Now think about the people in your network. Who do you know who has these traits? Do you already have a relationship with this person? If not, can you reach out to him or her? Use the following worksheet to write down a few possible candidates.

Possible Mentors

List three people who could guide you in your career development, along with their contact information.

Mentor 1

Name: _____

Title: _____

Organization: _____

Address: _____

Phone Number: _____ E-mail: _____

Mentor 2

Name: _____

Title: _____

Organization: _____

Address: _____

Phone Number: _____ E-mail: _____

Mentor 3

Name: _____

Title: _____

Organization: _____

Address: _____

Phone Number: _____ E-mail: _____

Choose to have a mentor because you want someone to give you honest, sometimes hard-to-hear advice on your own career. You want someone you can talk to about trouble you're having with a current boss or co-worker. You want someone who will help you see your own faults or areas to improve. You want someone who already has a network of people in the job area you want to work. You want someone who will make you go beyond the limits you've set for yourself. This person will help you grow.

Have a Life Outside of Work

The final part of positioning yourself to get ahead is to continue your hobbies, sports, and other interests you enjoy when you are not working. Doing so makes you a balanced person and can actually strengthen your skills and ability to perform well on the job and have an enduring, rewarding career.

Your Plan for Continuing the Hobbies and Interests You Enjoy

In the following worksheet, list your hobbies, sports, and other interests. Then create a schedule that allows you time to continue pursuing those in your free time.

Interest	Time(s) Set Aside to Concentrate on the Interest
_____	_____
_____	_____
_____	_____
_____	_____
_____	_____

Look for Ways to Enjoy Your Work

Knowing all the right people and getting all the best advice others give you won't help you if your work makes you unhappy. Truly enjoying what you're doing affects everything—from your attitude to your upward mobility.

Here are some actions you can take to keep you satisfied with your job:

- **Be positive.** Look for things you like about your job. Avoid saying negative things to others, particularly co-workers, about your work. And spend your time with positive people, on and off the job.

- **Let your supervisor know you care about your performance within the organization.** Meet with your supervisor every few months to review your progress. Indicate that you want to succeed and ask for advice on what you can do to get a promotion, increase in pay, or some other goal. Keep track of your progress and review it with your supervisor on a regular basis.

- **Volunteer for new assignments.** If you have mastered your job, let your supervisor know you want to take on additional tasks. This way you can learn new skills, maintain interest in the job, and let your supervisor know you are able to handle more.

- **Transfer to a new job at the same organization.** Look for opportunities within your organization to move into another job opening that interests you more, has higher pay, or more opportunities than the one you have now.

- **Teach or mentor others.** Teaching or mentoring co-workers is a valuable skill, so look for chances to do this. For example, you may want to ask your supervisor to assign you the responsibility for orienting new staff.

- **Ask for what you want.** Others may not know the direction you want to take your career. It's up to you to let them know by asking them for what you want.

When Things Don't Work Out

In some cases, you may not get what you want or need from your job. Your supervisor or co-workers may be difficult to work with, or you may not see a chance to meet your career goals. If so, you should consider looking elsewhere for a position that brings you fulfillment. Before you leave your current position, make sure that

- You know and follow the procedure for leaving a job.
- You have another job.
- That new job is a better position, one in which you will be making more money, enjoy the work more, or get along with your co-workers and supervisors better—or all of these.

If you do decide to leave your current job, do not discuss this negatively with your co-workers or supervisor. Continue to be respectful, efficient, and dependable even as you search for a different job. That way, your supervisor or others will be comfortable in recommending you to others.

If your employer is the one who decides that you should leave, go quietly and quickly, if required. Nothing is gained by arguing or complaining.

In Conclusion

Beginning a new job or staying in one that is less than perfect can be a real challenge. We hope the information in this booklet has been helpful to you and that it will prove even more valuable as you grow in your career. We know that you will be rewarded for taking the time and effort you exerted to read the booklet and complete its worksheets.

All the best.

The Editors at JIST

Mike Farr

Appendix A

Your Career Plan Worksheet

Every minute you spend mapping out a career path is time well spent, even if life brings unexpected changes or your personal growth leads you in other directions. Following is a worksheet in which you can transfer the plans you began in the preceding pages of this booklet or write entirely new ones to reflect where you are today.

CAREER PLAN WORKSHEET

Take some time to complete this worksheet carefully. It will help you create a career plan you can use for many years. Use an erasable pen or pencil to allow for changes and corrections. Use extra sheets of paper as needed.

Name _____

Ultimate Career Goal _____

A Positive Habit I Want to Develop

1. A habit I want to create is _____

2. My payoff for developing the habit is _____

3. In order to develop this habit, I must make these changes:

   a. _____

   b. _____

   c. _____

   d. _____

   e. _____

(continued)

(continued)

A Skill I Want to Acquire

1. A skill I want to acquire is _____

   _____

2. To learn that skill or get more training, I will _____

   _____

3. The date by which I plan to have gained that skill is _____

The Additional Education I Want to Acquire

1. The additional education I want to acquire is _____

   _____

2. I plan to get that education at _____

   _____

3. The date by which I plan to have completed that education is

   _____

4. The steps I need to take in order to do that are

   a. _____

   b. _____

   c. _____

Contact Information for the People in My Network

Name	E-mail Address	Phone Number
_____	_____	_____
_____	_____	_____
_____	_____	_____
_____	_____	_____
_____	_____	_____

My Five-Year Career Plan

Year 1

1. My goal for this year is _____
   _____

2. To achieve that goal, I must take the following incremental steps:

   a. _____

   b. _____

   c. _____

Year 2

1. My goal for Year 2 is _____
   _____

2. To achieve that goal, I must take the following incremental steps:

   a. _____

   b. _____

   c. _____

Year 3

1. My goal for Year 3 is _____
   _____

2. To achieve that goal, I must take the following incremental steps:

   a. _____

   b. _____

   c. _____

Year 4

1. My goal for Year 4 is _____
   _____

(continued)

(continued)

2. To achieve that goal, I must take the following incremental steps:

   a. _____

   b. _____

   c. _____

Year 5

1. My goal for Year 5 is _____

   _____

2. To achieve that goal, I must take the following incremental steps:

   a. _____

   b. _____

   c. _____

Congratulations! You have taken the time to plan one of the most important parts of your life. You won't regret it. Now you are ready to put those plans into action. All the best to you!

> To accomplish great things, we must not only act, but also dream; not only plan, but also believe.
>
> *Anatole France*

> If you have built castles in the air, your work need not be lost; that is where they should be. Now put the foundations under them.
>
> *Henry David Thoreau*

Appendix B

Additional Sources of Information

Thousands of books and countless Internet sites provide information on resumes, cover letters, and job success subjects. Space limitations do not permit us to describe the many good resources available, so we just listed some of the most useful ones. Because this is our list, we've included books Michael Farr wrote or JIST publishes. You should be able to find these and many other resources at libraries, bookstores, and Web bookselling sites such as Amazon.com.

Books with Information on Job Success

Here are a few good books that include information on being a success at work: *Job Savvy: How to Be a Success at Work,* Third Edition, by LaVerne L. Ludden, Ed.D., is a workbook that gives in-depth information about basic workplace skills, including keeping a job and getting ahead. *How to Be Happy at Work* by Arlene S. Hirsch uses real-life stories and case studies to address common obstacles to career fulfillment. *First-Job Survival Guide: How to Thrive and Advance in Your New Career* by Victoria A. Hoevemeyer, Diane C. Decker, and Marianne Rowe-Dimas is a unique, easy-to-read reference guide that reveals the secrets for getting along and getting ahead at work. *Career Success Is Color-Blind: Overcoming Prejudice and Eliminating Barriers in the Workplace*, Second Edition, by Ollie Stevenson gives comprehensive, sound advice to help individuals of diverse racial or cultural backgrounds achieve success within mainstream America.

Resume and Cover Letter Books

Michael Farr books. If you'd like additional information on resumes and cover letters, check out Michael Farr's book *The Quick Resume & Cover Letter Book,* one of the top-selling resume books at various large bookstore chains. It is very simple to follow, is inexpensive, has good design, and has good sample resumes written by professional resume writers. For more in-depth but still quick help, check out his two books in the Help in a Hurry series: *Same-Day Resume* (with advice on creating a simple resume in an hour and a better one later) and *15-Minute Cover Letter,* co-authored with Louise Kursmark (offering a gallery of sample cover letters and tips for writing them fast and effectively).

Other books published by JIST. The following titles include many sample resumes written by professional resume writers, as well as good advice: *Amazing Resumes* by Jim Bright and Joanne Earl; *Cover Letter Magic* by Wendy S. Enelow and Louise M. Kursmark; the entire Expert Resumes series by Enelow and Kursmark; *Federal Resume Guidebook* by Kathryn Kraemer Troutman; *Gallery of Best Resumes, Gallery of Best Cover Letters,* and *Gallery of Best Resumes for People Without a Four-Year Degree* by David F. Noble; and *Résumé Magic* by Susan Britton Whitcomb.

Internet Resources

There are too many Web sites to list in this appendix, but you can start at the JIST Web site, www.jist.com, for lists of recommended sites for career, education, and related topics, along with comments on each.

Be aware that some Web sites provide poor advice, so ask your librarian, instructor, or counselor for suggestions on those best for your needs.

Other Resources

Libraries. Most libraries have the books mentioned here, as well as many other resources. Many also provide Internet access so that you can research online information. Ask the librarian for help finding what you need.

People. People who hold the jobs that interest you are excellent career information sources. Ask them what they like and don't like about their work, how they got started, and the education or training they needed. Most people are helpful and will give advice you can't get any other way.

Career Counseling. A good vocational counselor can help you explore career options. Take advantage of this service if it is available to you. Also consider a career-planning course or program, which will encourage you to be more thorough in your thinking.

Appendix C

Use a Portfolio to Keep a Record of Your Career

Your resume is impressive, but there is another way that you can collect evidence of who you are and what you can do—a career portfolio.

What Is a Career Portfolio?

Unlike a resume, a career portfolio is a collection of documents that can include a variety of items. Here are some items you may want to place in your portfolio:

- Resume
- School transcripts
- Summary of skills
- Credentials, such as diplomas and certificates of recognition
- Reference letters from school officials and instructors, former employers, or co-workers
- List of accomplishments: Describe hobbies and interests that are not directly related to your job objective and are not included on your resume.
- Examples of your work: Depending on your career, you can include samples of your artwork, photographs of a project, audiotapes, videotapes, images of Web pages you developed, and other media that can provide examples of your work.

Place each item on a separate page when you assemble your career portfolio.

Create a Digital Portfolio

A digital portfolio, also known as an electronic portfolio, contains all the information from your career portfolio in an electronic format. This material is then copied onto a CD-ROM or published on a Web site. With a digital portfolio, you can present your skills to a greater number of people than you can your paper career portfolio.

YOUR CAREER PORTFOLIO

On the following lines, list the items you want to include in your career portfolio. Think specifically of those items that show your skills, education, and personal accomplishments.

_____
_____
_____
_____
_____
_____
_____
_____
_____
_____
_____
_____
_____
_____
_____
_____
_____
_____
_____
_____
_____
_____
_____
_____
_____